Lear

For Kids

Numbers, Poems, Riddles, Colors and Shapes, Short Stories and Jokes; My Best Haitian Kreyòl Book Ever

Jonathan K Rico

Copyright

Table Of Contents

Introduction

About the Book

Welcome, dear friends, to a magical journey where words form bridges between worlds, and sounds paint colors of a vibrant culture. "Learn Haitian Creole for Kids" is not just a book; it's a treasure chest filled with the rich and melodious language of Haiti, waiting for you to unlock its secrets.

Have you ever wanted to speak like the heroes of Haitian tales, or count like the great market vendors in Port-au-Prince? Or perhaps, you've dreamed of solving riddles that have been whispered under the Caribbean stars for generations? If your heart says "yes," then you're in the right place!

This book is your map to a land of numbers, poems, riddles, short stories, and jokes—all in Haitian Creole. Whether you're a brave toddler setting sail on your first language adventure, a curious child ready to explore new words, or a champion reader eager to master the musical rhythm of Kreyol, there's something here for everyone.

As we embark on this journey together, you'll meet funny characters, solve mysteries with clever riddles, and laugh at jokes that will make your belly jiggle like a bowl full of jelly. And the best part? You'll be learning Haitian Creole all along the way.

So, grab your explorer's hat, and let's dive into the pages that lie ahead. Remember, every page you turn opens a door to a new adventure. Are you ready to discover the wonders of Haitian Creole? Let the adventure begin!

Why Learn Haitian Creole?

Imagine being able to whisper "hello" in a language that dances like a breeze through the mountains of Haiti, or to share a secret joke that sparkles like the Caribbean sea. Haitian Creole, or Kreyòl as it's lovingly called, is a language of stories, laughter, and community. It's a key that unlocks the heart of a rich culture and connects us to millions of people.

Here's why learning Haitian Creole is a fantastic journey to embark on:

- **Unlock a World of Culture:** Haiti is a land of vibrant festivals, mesmerizing music, and compelling history. By learning Kreyòl, you'll gain a passport to this cultural richness, understanding the stories and songs in the way they were meant to be shared.

- **Make New Friends:** Speaking Haitian Creole opens up opportunities to meet new friends and connect with Haitian communities, whether you're in Haiti, parts of the United States, or other corners of the globe where Haitians have brought their indomitable spirit.
- **Boost Your Brain Power:** Learning a new language is like a super workout for your brain. It improves memory, enhances problem-solving skills, and even makes you a better listener. And what's cooler than having a super-brain?
- **Be a Bridge Builder:** In our wonderfully diverse world, being bilingual (or multilingual!) helps you become a bridge between cultures, promoting understanding and empathy. By speaking Haitian Creole, you can help bring people together in a beautiful way.

- **Have Fun!:** Last but not least, learning Haitian Creole is fun! The language is full of expressions, sounds, and rhythms that are joyful to speak. You'll enjoy every giggle-inducing mistake, every triumphant conversation, and every moment of connection.

So, are you ready to leap into the delightful adventure of learning Haitian Creole? Let's turn the page and dive into a world where every word is a step on a journey, and every sentence brings us closer together. Welcome aboard, young explorers!

Numbers

Counting from 1 to 10

Let's embark on our first adventure into the world of Haitian Creole by learning how to count from 1 to 10. Each number is a step on our path, leading us to new discoveries and friends. Are you ready to count with me? Here we go!

1. **Enn** (en) - Imagine ONE drum beating in the heart of a festive parade. Can you tap your chest **one** time like the drum?
2. **De** (deh) - TWO hands clapping to the rhythm of the music. Clap your hands **twice** for the joy of dance!
3. **Twa** (twah) - THREE birds flying high in the sky. Flap your

arms **three** times and soar with them!

4. **Kat** (kaht) - FOUR stars twinkling in the night sky. Blink your eyes **four** times to make the stars shine.

5. **Senk** (sank) - FIVE colorful fruits in a basket. Can you pretend to eat **five** delicious fruits?

6. **Sis** (sees) - SIX fish swimming in the sea. Swim with your arms **six** times through the waves.

7. **Sèt** (set) - SEVEN leaves dancing in the breeze. Shake your body **seven** times with the leaves.

8. **Uit** (weet) - EIGHT stones paving a path to adventure. Tap your feet **eight** times as you walk the path.

9. **Nèf** (nef) - NINE stars lighting up the night. Shine your hands

outwards **nine** times to light up the dark.

10.   **Dis** (dees) - TEN happy children playing together. Jump up and down **ten** times with happiness!

Let's Practice!

Now that we've learned to count from 1 to 10 in Haitian Creole, let's practice together. Can you find **ten** things in your room to count? Use your new skills to count them out loud in Haitian Creole!

Numbers in Everyday Life

Now that we've learned how to count from 1 to 10 in Haitian Creole, let's discover how these numbers show up in our everyday lives. Numbers are everywhere, from the pages of a book to the petals on a flower. They help us share stories, solve mysteries, and celebrate the world around us. Let's explore how numbers weave into our daily adventures!

1. Enn for One Sun in the Sky

Every morning, **one** sun rises, filling the day with light and warmth. Can you say "enn solèy" (one sun) when you wake up and see the sun greeting you?

2. De for Two Feet that Walk and Dance

You walk and dance on **two** feet. When you take steps or dance to a beat, remember "de pye" (two feet) carrying you through your day.

3. Twa for Three Meals a Day

Breakfast, lunch, and dinner - **three** meals that keep you healthy and strong. Next mealtime, can you count "twa manje" (three meals)?

4. Kat for Four Seasons

Spring, summer, fall, and winter - **four** seasons that paint our year with different colors and feelings. What season is it now? Can you find "kat sezon" (four seasons) outside?

5. Senk for Five Fingers to Play and Create

With **five** fingers on each hand, you can draw, write, and play. Look at your hands and wiggle "senk dwèt" (five fingers).

6. Sis for Six Colors of the Rainbow

Red, orange, yellow, green, blue, and purple - the **six** colors that make a rainbow. After the rain, search for a "sis koulè lakansyèl" (six-color rainbow).

7. Sèt for Seven Days of the Week

Each week has **seven** days, filled with learning, playing, and exploring. Can you name the days of the week in Haitian Creole?

8. Uit for Eight Notes in Music

Music comes alive with **eight** basic notes, creating songs and melodies. Listen to a song and imagine the "uit nòt" (eight notes) dancing in the air.

9. Nèf for Nine Planets in the Solar System

Our solar system has **nine** planets, each orbiting the sun in space. Can you imagine traveling through space and visiting "nèf planèt" (nine planets)?

10. Dis for Ten Toes to Explore the World

Your **ten** toes help you stand, walk, and explore the world around you. Wiggle your "dis zòtèy" (ten toes) and think of where they might take you next!

Let's Play a Game!

Can you find examples of each number in your home or outside? Use your new Haitian Creole counting skills to identify numbers in your everyday life. This game helps you practice counting and connects your learning to the world around you. Have fun discovering numbers everywhere!

Fun Number Games

Let's put our counting skills to the test with some fun number games! These activities are perfect for practicing Haitian Creole numbers and can be played anywhere - at home, in the park, or even during a car ride. Ready, set, let's count and play!

1. Treasure Hunt

- **How to Play:** Hide small objects around your home or classroom.
- **Objective:** Find the objects, but there's a twist! You can only pick them up if you can count to the number on a note nearby in Haitian Creole. For example, if you find a note with "kat" (four), you need to say "enn, de, twa, kat" before collecting the treasure.

2. Number Tag

- **How to Play:** This is like the classic game of tag, but with a numerical twist.

- **Objective:** When "it" tags someone, they must freeze and shout a number in Haitian Creole. To be unfrozen, another player must touch them and count to that number in Haitian Creole.

3. Count and Jump

- **How to Play:** Create a simple hopscotch layout with numbers from 1 to 10 written in each box.
- **Objective:** Jump through the hopscotch, but instead of skipping boxes, the challenge is to say each number in Haitian Creole as you land on it. See if you can make it to "dis" (ten) without missing a number!

4. Musical Numbers

- **How to Play:** Play music and have everyone dance around. When the music stops, call out a number in Haitian Creole.

- **Objective:** The players must quickly form groups of that size. Anyone who isn't in a group when they're all formed is out. Keep playing until one winner remains.

5. Number Drawing

- **How to Play:** With paper and crayons, draw simple objects or animals.
- **Objective:** Beside each drawing, write how many of that thing you've drawn, but in Haitian Creole numbers. For example, if you draw three cats, write "twa chat" beside them. Share your art and practice counting what you've drawn with friends or family.

Remember to Play and Learn

Playing these games is not just about winning; it's about practicing your new language skills and having fun. Each time you play, you'll get better at counting in

Haitian Creole. So, don't be afraid to make mistakes—that's part of learning! The most important thing is to enjoy the journey and celebrate every step forward with a smile and a high five.

Happy counting, and may each game bring you closer to becoming a counting champion in Haitian Creole!

Poems

Traditional Haitian Creole Poems

1. The Mango Tree

Under the mango tree, we play, In the shade, we laugh and sway. Sweet mangoes high above, Gifts from the sky, sent with love.

"Mango dous, mango dous," we sing, Happiness and laughter they bring. In the breeze, the leaves do dance, Under the mango tree, we take our chance.

To climb, to reach, to taste the sweet, Mangoes in our hands, a joyful treat. "Mango dous, mango dous," all day, Under the mango tree, we love to stay.

2. The Little Frog (Ti Krapo)

Ti krapo by the river side, Singing his song with pride. "Kwak kwak kwak," he sings so clear, A song of rain, for all to hear.

Jumping high, jumping far, Ti krapo is a star. In the moonlight, he leaps and plays, Singing his rainy day praise.

So listen well when rain is near, Ti krapo's song, you'll surely hear. "Kwak kwak kwak," a melody so bright, Thanking the rain, into the night.

3. Stars Over Haiti (Zetwal Ayiti)

Look up high, what do you see? Stars over Haiti, shining free. Each one a story, an ancient tale, Of love and courage, that never grows stale.

"Zetwal Ayiti, zetwal Ayiti," Whisper their names, feel the magic ignite. Guiding us through, the night so deep, Under their watch, we peacefully sleep.

So when the night sky, you come to greet, Remember the stories, ever so sweet.

"Zetwal Ayiti, zetwal Ayiti," In their light, we are never alone, Together under the vast, starlit dome.

Poems for Learning Vocabulary

1. In My Garden (Nan Jaden Mwen)

In my garden, what do I see?
Nan jaden mwen, kisa m wè?
Flowers blooming, pretty and bright,
Flè k ap fleri, bèl ak klere,
Butterflies dancing, what a sight!
Papiyon k ap danse, ki bel bagay!

I see a **kat** (four) leaf clover,
Mwen wè yon kat fèy klèv,
And **senk** (five) bees buzzing over.
E senk myèl k ap bourdonnen.
In my garden, life's a song,
Nan jaden mwen, lavi se yon chante,
Join me and sing along.
Vini avè m epi chante ansanm.

2. The Colors of the Day (Koulè Jou a)

The sun rises, **jòn** (yellow) and warm,
Solèy la leve, jòn e cho,
A new day, a new dawn is born.
Yon nouvo jou, yon nouvo lòtbò a fèt.

The sky turns **ble** (blue), wide and clear,
Syèl la vin ble, laj e klè,
Clouds like cotton, floating near.
Nwaj tankou koton, ap flote toupre.

Vèt (green) trees wave in the light,
Pyebwa vèt ap balanse nan limyè a,
Birds sing, taking flight.
Zwazo ap chante, yo pran vòl.

As evening comes, the sky glows **wouj** (red),
Lè aswè a rive, syèl la klere wouj,
Stars peek, it's time for bed.
Zetwal yo kòmanse parèt, li lè pou dòmi.

3. My Family (Fanmi Mwen)

Manman (mother) hugs me tight,
Manman sere mwen fò,

Her love a guiding light.
Lanmou li se yon limyè gid.

Papa (father) teaches me to play,
Papa moutre mwen jwe,
With him, I'd spend all day.
Avè l, mwen ta pase tout jounen an.

My **sè** (sister) and I share our toys,
Mwen ak sè mwen pataje jwèt nou yo,
Creating worlds, imagining joys.
Nou kreye mond, imajine kè kontan.

With my **frè** (brother), I explore,
Avèk frè mwen, mwen eksplore,
Learning, laughing, always more.
Aprann, ri, toujou gen plis.

Riddles

Easy Riddles for Kids

Riddles in English

1. What has a heart that doesn't beat?
2. What can travel all around the world without leaving its corner?
3. What has keys but can't open a single lock?
4. What comes down but never goes up?
5. I'm tall when I'm young, and I'm short when I'm old. What am I?
6. What is full of holes but still holds water?
7. What can you catch, but not throw?
8. What has a head, a tail, is brown, and has no legs?
9. What gets wetter as it dries?
10. What has words, but never speaks?

Written in Haitian Creole

1. Kisa ki gen yon kè men ki pa janm bat?
2. Kisa ki ka vwayaje toupatou nan mond lan san li pa kite kwen li?
3. Kisa ki gen kle men ki pa ka louvri okenn kadna?
4. Kisa ki desann men ki pa janm monte?
5. Mwen wo lè mwen jèn, e mwen kout lè mwen vyeyi. Kisa mwen ye?
6. Kisa ki plen twou men ki toujou kenbe dlo?
7. Kisa ou ka pran, men ou pa ka voye?
8. Kisa ki gen tèt, yon ke, li mawon, epi li pa gen janm?
9. Kisa ki vin pi mouye pandan li ap sèch?
10. Kisa ki gen mo, men ki janm palc?

Answers

1. **A tree (Yon pyebwa)**
2. **A stamp (Yon timb)**
3. **A piano (Yon pyano)**

4. **Rain (Lapli)**
5. **A candle (Yon chandèl)**
6. **A sponge (Yon eponj)**
7. **A cold (Yon grip)**
8. **A coin (Yon pyès monnen)**
9. **A towel (Yon sèvyèt)**
10. **A book (Yon liv)**

Challenging Riddles to Sharpen the Mind

Challenging Riddles in English

1. I speak without a voice and listen without ears. I have no body, but I come alive with the wind. What am I?
2. The more of this there is, the less you see. What is it?
3. I start with the letter 'E', end with the letter 'E', but only contain one letter. What am I?
4. I am not alive, but I grow; I don't have lungs, but I need air; I don't have a mouth, but water kills me. What am I?
5. Forward I am heavy, but backward I am not. What am I?
6. What has cities, but no houses; forests, but no trees; and rivers, but no water?

7. What goes up and down, but always remains in the same place?
8. You see a boat filled with people. It has not sunk, but when you look again, you don't see a single person on the boat. Why?
9. I am always hungry and will die if not fed, but if you water me, I'll die. What am I?
10. What can run but never walks, has a mouth but never talks, has a head but never weeps, has a bed but never sleeps?

Written in Haitian Creole

1. Mwen pale san vwa e mwen koute san zòrèy. Mwen pa gen kò, men mwen vin vivan ak van an. Kisa mwen ye?

2. Plis ou genyen sa, mwens ou wè. Kisa li ye?

3. Mwen kòmanse ak lèt 'E', fini ak lèt 'E', men mwen sèlman genyen yon lèt. Kisa mwen ye?

4. Mwen pa vivan, men mwen grandi; mwen pa gen poumon, men mwen bezwen lè; mwen pa gen bouch, men dlo touye m. Kisa mwen ye?

5. Devan mwen lou, men dèyè mwen pa. Kisa mwen ye?

6. Kisa ki gen vil, men pa gen kay; gen forè, men pa gen pyebwa; e gen rivyè, men pa gen dlo?

7. Kisa ki monte e desann, men toujou rete nan menm plas la?

8. Ou wè yon bato chaje ak moun. Li pa koule, men lè ou gade ankò, ou pa wè yon sèl moun sou bato a. Poukisa?

9. Mwen toujou grangou e m ap mouri si m pa jwenn manje, men si ou ba m dlo, mwen ap mouri. Kisa mwen ye?

10.   Kisa ki ka kouri men ki pa janm mache, gen bouch men pa janm pale, gen tèt men pa janm kriye, gen kabann men pa janm dòmi?

Answers

1. **An Echo (Yon ekò)**
2. **Darkness (Fènwa)**
3. **An Envelope (Yon anvlòp)**
4. **Fire (Dife)**
5. **The word 'ton' (Mo 'ton')**
6. **A Map (Yon kat jeyografik)**
7. **Stairs (Eskalye)**
8. **All the people were married (Tout moun yo te marye)** — not a single person.
9. **Fire (Dife)**
10. **A River (Yon rivyè)**

Short Stories

Folktales from Haiti

Bouki and Ti Malice

Bouki and Ti Malice are two of the most iconic characters in Haitian folklore, representing the eternal interplay between guile and wit. Bouki, often portrayed as a somewhat slow-witted but strong individual, is frequently outsmarted by the clever and cunning Ti Malice. In one popular tale, Ti Malice invites Bouki to share a meal but devises a scheme to eat all the food himself. This story, like many others featuring the duo, ends with Ti Malice outwitting Bouki, serving as a humorous reminder of the value of sharp wit and intelligence.

The Magic Orange Tree

The Magic Orange Tree is a beloved Haitian folktale about a young girl who, after being mistreated by her stepmother, discovers a magical orange tree that fulfills her wishes. The tale highlights themes of kindness, resilience, and justice, as the girl's good heart leads her to share the fruits of the tree with those in need, eventually leading to her liberation from hardship. This story is often told to teach children about the rewards of generosity and the importance of facing adversity with courage.

Tezen

Tezen is a poignant tale about loyalty and love, centered around a beautiful fish that forms a deep bond with a young girl. This folktale delves into themes of sacrifice, the connection between humans and nature, and the transformative power of love. Tezen, in many versions, is a magical fish that is actually a spirit or a transformed human being who provides assistance or guidance to the protagonist, often leading to a narrative that explores the depth of friendship and the mysteries of the natural world.

The Children of the Moon

The Children of the Moon is a mystical story that explains the origins of mosquitoes. According to the tale, mosquitoes were once human beings cursed by the moon for their greed and dishonesty. This story serves as a cautionary tale about the consequences of negative traits such as greed, envy, and deceit, teaching children the value of honesty and integrity.

Why the Sea is Salty

Why the Sea is Salty is a folktale that explains a natural phenomenon through the story of a magical mill that grinds out whatever its owner wishes. The tale usually ends in tragedy or moral lesson when the mill, having been set to grind out salt, is lost at sea and continues to grind salt forever, making the sea salty. This story teaches about the dangers of greed and the importance of understanding and respecting the power of nature.

Moral Stories for Character Development

1. The Boy Who Cried Wolf

Lesson: Honesty and Trust
A shepherd boy repeatedly tricks nearby villagers into thinking a wolf is attacking his flock. When a wolf actually appears and he calls for help, the villagers believe it's another false alarm and ignore him, leading to a devastating loss. This story teaches the importance of honesty and the consequences of lying, highlighting how trust is difficult to rebuild once broken.

2. The Tortoise and the Hare

Lesson: Perseverance and Humility
In this classic fable, a slow but steady tortoise wins a race against a fast but overconfident hare. The hare, believing he could easily outpace the tortoise, decides to rest mid-race and falls asleep, while the

tortoise continues on and finishes the race first. This story emphasizes the value of perseverance, consistent effort, and humility over arrogance and complacency.

3. The Ant and the Grasshopper

Lesson: Responsibility and Planning for the   Future
The ant works hard all summer to store food for the winter, while the grasshopper wastes time and mocks the ant's efforts. Come winter, the grasshopper is hungry and regretful, while the ant is well-prepared and comfortable. This tale teaches the importance of responsibility, hard work, and preparing for the future rather than succumbing to instant gratification.

4. Stone Soup

Lesson: Cooperation and the Value of Sharing
A group of hungry travelers arrives in a village, carrying nothing but an empty pot. They fill it with water and a stone and

manage to convince the villagers to each share a little bit of their food to help improve the soup's flavor. The result is a delicious meal for the entire village. This story highlights the benefits of cooperation and sharing, demonstrating how community and generosity can create abundance from scarcity.

5. The Lion and the Mouse

Lesson: Kindness and Gratitude
A mouse inadvertently wakes a lion, who initially threatens to eat it. The mouse begs for mercy and later returns the favor by freeing the lion from a poacher's net. This fable teaches that no act of kindness, however small, is ever wasted. It also illustrates how anyone, regardless of size or strength, can make a significant impact.

6. The Giving Tree

Lesson: Selflessness and Unconditional Love
This story follows the lifelong relationship

between a boy and a tree. The tree gives the boy everything she has to make him happy, even at great cost to herself. This touching narrative explores themes of selflessness, the nature of giving, and unconditional love, prompting reflections on generosity and gratitude.

Jokes

Silly Jokes to Make You Laugh

1. **Why don't eggs tell jokes?**
   They'd crack each other up!
2. **Why did the math book look sad?**
   Because it had too many problems.
3. **What do you call fake spaghetti?**
   An impasta!
4. **How do you organize a space party?**
   You planet.
5. **Why couldn't the bicycle stand up by itself?**
   It was two-tired.
6. **What did one wall say to the other wall?**
   "I'll meet you at the corner!"
7. **What do you call cheese that isn't yours?**
   Nacho cheese!

8. **Why did the scarecrow win an award?**

   Because he was outstanding in his field!

9. **What did the grape say when it got stepped on?**

   Nothing, it just let out a little wine!

10. **Why don't skeletons fight each other?**

    They don't have the guts.

11. **What do you call an alligator in a vest?**

    An investigator!

12. **Why did the tomato turn red?**

    Because it saw the salad dressing!

Knock-Knock Jokes in Haitian Creole

1. In English:

Knock,	**knock.**
Who's	there?
Lettuce.	
Lettuce	who?
Lettuce in, it's cold out here!	

1. in Kreyòl Ayisyen:

Tòk,		**tòk.**
Ki	moun	la?
Lètis.		
Lètis	ki	moun?
Lètis antre, fè frèt deyò a!		

2. In English

Knock,	**knock.**
Who's	there?
Atch.	

Atch		who?
Bless you!		

2. In Kreyòl Ayisyen:

Tòk,		**tòk.**
Ki	moun	la?
Atch.		
Atch	ki	moun?
Benediksyon!		

3. In English:

Knock,		**knock.**
Who's		there?
Olive.		
Olive		who?
Olive you and I miss you!		

3. In Kreyòl Ayisyen:

Tòk,		**tòk.**
Ki	moun	la?
Oliva.		
Oliva	ki	moun?
Oliva ou e mwen sonje ou!		

4. In English:

Knock,   **knock.**
Who's   there?
Cow   **says.**
Cow   says   who?
No, cow says moooo!

4. In Kreyòl Ayisyen:

Tòk,   **tòk.**
Ki   moun   la?
Vach   **di.**
Vach   di   ki   moun?
Non, vach di mmmmm!

5. In English:

Knock,   **knock.**
Who's   there?
Harry.
Harry   who?
Harry up and answer the door!

5. In Kreyòl Ayisyen:

Tòk, **tòk.**

Ki moun la?

Ari.

Ari ki moun?

Ari prese reponn pòt la!

Vocabulary Building

Everyday Words and Phrases

Greetings and Basic Politeness

- **Hello:** Bonjou (in the morning), Bonswa (in the evening)
- **Goodbye:** Orevwa
- **Please:** Tanpri
- **Thank you:** Mèsi
- **Yes:** Wi
- **No:** Non
- **Excuse me / Sorry:** Eskize m

Common Questions and Responses

- **How are you?:** Kòman ou ye?
  - **I'm good, thank you:** Mwen byen, mèsi.
- **What's your name?:** Kijan ou rele?
  - **My name is...:** Mwen rele...
- **Where are you from?:** Ki kote ou soti?

- ○ **I'm from...:** Mwen soti nan...

Everyday Activities

- **I'm hungry:** Mwen grangou
- **I'm thirsty:** Mwen swaf
- **I'm tired:** Mwen fatige
- **Let's go:** Ann ale
- **I understand:** Mwen konprann
- **I don't understand:** Mwen pa konprann

Shopping and Dining

- **How much is this?:** Konbyen sa a koute?
- **I would like...:** Mwen ta renmen...
- **The bill, please:** Bill la, tanpri
- **Water:** Dlo
- **Food:** Manje
- **Restaurant:** Restoran

Emergency and Health

- **Help!:** Ede!
- **I need a doctor:** Mwen bezwen yon doktè

- **Where is the bathroom?:** Kote twalèt la?

Expressing Feelings

- **I like it:** Mwen renmen li
- **I don't like it:** Mwen pa renmen li
- **I'm happy:** Mwen kontan
- **I'm sad:** Mwen tris

Learning Colors, Shapes, and Sizes

Colors (Koulè)

- **Red:** Wouj (rooj)
- **Blue:** Ble (bleh)
- **Green:** Vèt (vehr)
- **Yellow:** Jon (joh)
- **Black:** Nwa (nwah)
- **White:** Blan (blah)
- **Orange:** Zoranj (zoh-rahj)
- **Purple:** Mòv (mohv)
- **Pink:** Woz (wohz)
- **Brown:** Mawon (mah-woh)

Shapes (Fòm)

- **Circle:** Sèk (sehk)
- **Square:** Kare (kah-reh)
- **Rectangle:** Rektang (rek-tahng)
- **Triangle:** Triyang (tree-yahng)
- **Star:** Zetwal (zet-wahl)
- **Heart:** Kè (keh)
- **Oval:** Oval (oh-val)

Sizes (Gwosè)

- **Big:** Gwo (gwoh)
- **Small:** Piti (pee-tee)
- **Tall:** Wo (woh)
- **Short (height):** Kout (koot)
- **Short (length):** Kout (koot)
- **Long:** Long (lohng)
- **Wide:** Laj (lahj)
- **Narrow:** Etwat (et-waht)
- **Thick:** Epè (eh-peh)
- **Thin:** Mens (mehns)

Example Sentences

1. **The red apple is big:** Pòm wouj la gwo. (Pohm rooj lah gwoh)
2. **A small blue car:** Yon ti machin ble. (Yohn tee ma-sheen bleh)
3. **The square is white:** Kare a blan. (Kah-reh ah blah)
4. **A long, thin road:** Yon wout long ak mens. (Yohn woot lohng ahk mehns)

Animals, Fruits, and Vegetables

Animals (Bèt)

- **Dog:** Chen (shen)
- **Cat:** Chat (sha)
- **Bird:** Zwazo (zwa-zo)
- **Fish:** Pwason (pwa-son)
- **Horse:** Cheval (she-val)
- **Cow:** Bèf (bef)
- **Goat:** Kabrit (ka-brit)
- **Chicken:** Poul (poul)
- **Pig:** Kochon (ko-shon)
- **Rabbit:** Lapen (la-pen)

Fruits (Fwi)

- **Apple:** Pòm (pohm)
- **Banana:** Bannann (ban-nan)
- **Orange:** Zoranj (zo-ranj)
- **Mango:** Mango (man-go)
- **Pineapple:** Anana (a-na-na)
- **Grape:** Rezen (re-zen)
- **Watermelon:** Melon dlo (me-lon dlo)
- **Papaya:** Papay (pa-pay)

- **Coconut:** Kokoye (ko-ko-ye)
- **Avocado:** Zaboka (za-bo-ka)

Vegetables (Legim)

- **Carrot:** Kawòt (ka-wot)
- **Onion:** Zonyon (zo-nyon)
- **Potato:** Pòmdetè (pohm-deh-teh)
- **Tomato:** Tomat (to-mat)
- **Cabbage:** Chou (shou)
- **Pepper:** Piman (pi-man)
- **Cucumber:** Konkonm (kon-kom)
- **Eggplant:** Berejenn (be-re-jenn)
- **Lettuce:** Lètis (leh-tis)
- **Spinach:** Epina (e-pi-na)

Example Sentences

- **I see a cat:** Mwen wè yon chat. (Mweh weh yohn sha)
- **I like to eat mango:** Mwen renmen manje mango. (Mweh renmen man-jeh man-go)
- **The rabbit is eating a carrot:** Lapen an ap manje yon kawòt. (La-pen ahn ap man-jeh yohn kawot)

Conclusion

And just like that, our journey through the vibrant world of Haitian Creole comes to a gentle close. With every page turned, we've danced through numbers, sung with poems, chuckled over riddles, and wandered through stories that warmed our hearts. Not to forget, the laughter shared with every silly joke that jumped out at us!

We ventured together, not just to learn, but to feel the joy of Haitian Creole, a language as colorful and welcoming as the island it calls home. From counting stars in the night sky to meeting creatures big and small, each word we've shared is a step closer to a world where language unites us all.

Remember, every number tells a story, every poem paints a picture, and every riddle is a key to a door waiting to be opened. And as for the stories and jokes, they're our companions, reminding us that learning is a journey filled with laughter, wonder, and the warmth of shared tales.

So, keep these lessons close to your heart. Let them be your guides as you explore, discover, and dream. For the world of Haitian Creole is a treasure chest, waiting for curious minds and eager hearts to unlock its riches.

Until our paths cross again, carry the magic of these words with you. May they light your way and bring joy to your days, just as sharing them has brought joy to mine.

Mèsi, my dear friends, for this delightful adventure. Let's say "see you later" (nap wè pita), for in the world of stories and languages, every ending is just the beginning of a new tale waiting to be told.

Made in United States
Troutdale, OR
05/24/2024

20105767R10037